The River Is Another Kind of Prayer

New & Selected Poems
by
Kristofer Collins

Kung Fu Treachery Press
Rancho Cucamonga, CA

Copyright © Kristofer Collins, 2019
First Edition 1 3 5 7 9 10 8 6 4 2
ISBN: 978-1-950380-77-0
LCCN: 2019955641

Design, edits and layout: John T. Keehan, Jr.
Title page image: Kristofer Collins
Author photo: Anna Johnson
All rights reserved. No part of this publication may be reproduced or transmitted in any form or by any means, electronic or mechanical, including photocopying, recording or by info retrieval system, without prior written permission from the author.

Grateful acknowledgment is made to the following journals and publications for giving my work a good home over the years: *After Happy Hour Review, BBT Zine, The Camel Saloon, Chiron Review, Free State Review, The Glassblock, The Holiday Cafe, Jerry Jazz Musician, The Lilliput Review, Nerve Cowboy, The New Yinzer, The Ohio Vintage Matchbook Company, Pittsburgh City Paper, Pittsburgh PostGazette, Pittsburgh Poetry Review, Pittsburgh Quarterly, Rusty Truck, Uppagus, Vox Populi, Winedrunk Sidewalk.*

Selected poems first appeared, some in different versions, in the following collections and anthologies: *King Everything* (Six Gallery Press), *The Liturgy of Streets* (Six Gallery Press), *The Book of Names* (Low Ghost Press), *Last Call* (Speed and Briscoe), *Pennsylvania Welcomes You* (Coleridge Street Books), *Local Conditions* (Coleridge Street Press), *Salsa Night at Hilo Town Tavern* (Hyacinth Girl Press), *Nasty Women & Bad Hombres: A Poetry Anthology* (Lascaux Editions), 5 Poems (Grackle & Crow Press).

Thank you to my family for their continued support, encouragement, and patience.

Thank you to Michael Simms for his thoughts and suggestions at every stage of this project.

Special thanks to John Grochalski and Scott Silsbe for their amazing poetry and the inspiration it has provided me for so many years.

TABLE OF CONTENTS

New Poems

A River for Huff / 1

Sanctuary / 2

The Saddest Marathon Station in West Virginia / 3

Words My Father Never Taught Me / 4

Erroll Garner at the Ace / 5

The Departed / 7

An Old Man Poem / 8

The Suicides of Paris / 9

Acts of Contrition / 10

Burning / 11

Graffiti / 12

Panther Hollow Inn (1992) / 13

Asylum / 14

The Mystery of Faith / 15

The Lie / 16

Apology to John Dorsey for Missing His Reading / 17

Looking at Hokusai's The Great Wave of Kanagawa / 18

My Father Was a Kind of Country Song / 19

Dreaming Still / 20

South of Pimlico / 21

The Skaters / 22

Almond Way / 23

Distraction / 24

Listening to James Taylor at 40 / 26

Trouble / 27

San Francisco / 29

Ida / 30

Hemingway's Cafe 7.10.18 / 31

Pouring Ketchup from a Fresh Bottle of Heinz 57 / 32

The Photograph of Jay Dantry at the Entrance
   to Jay's Book Stall / 33

Bunny's Hasty Tasty Pancake House, Dayton, OH / 35

North Beach Offering / 36

This Train Won't Run / 37

John Lee Hooker in Juneau / 38

This Vicious Year / 39

Never Let Go / 41

Our Li Po / 42

Apology / 43

Home / 44

The Rumproller / 45

Selected Poems

A Poem for Jeff Who Is Far Away / 49

Fifth Avenue Poem / 50

Denver Poem / 51

Pittsburgh / 52

Coleridge Street, December Ninth / 53

Poem for Yvonne DeCarlo / 54

A Poem for Jessica / 55

Gelsomina / 56

After Patchen / 57

Nights at The Cage / 58

Ray's Marlin Grill with Scott Silsbe / 60

Ciao Marcello / 62

Bloomfield Bridge Tavern, Tuesday, 7:26pm / 63

Silky's Pub, Sunday, 2:10pm / 64

Poem for Dr. Harry J. Mooney / 65

The Last Call / 66

The Pittsburgh Baedeker / 67

June 16th, June 16th / 68

Poem Addressed to Jaquelyn Seigle / 69

BBT / 70

Some Morning / 71

The Whiskey Rebellion / 72

Baltimore / 73

Dawn Powell's Diaries / 75

For Robert Frank / 76

Poem for Anna / 77

Pedestrian Ceremony / 78

After Too Many Beers with Baldinger / 79

W. Eugene Smith / 80

Congress Avenue Bridge, Austin, TX / 81

Poem Addressed to Jonathan Moody / 83

Stanton Heights / 84

12 E. Read St. / 85

I Am Not Kahlil Gibran / 86

The Old Stories / 87

Heaven / 88

Fix Bayonets / 89

Ruth / 90

Mannish Boy / 91

Good Noise / 92

Identifying Trees / 93

Summer Town / 94

On John Cheever's First Listening to Joni Mitchell's
   The Last Time I Saw Richard / 95

Poem for M. Callen / 96

Old Women and Their Old Dogs / 97

Omar Moreno / 98

Celica / 99

My Mother Looked Like Stevie Nicks / 100

Yinz / 101

A Belated Poem for My Wife's 30th Birthday / 102

Salsa Night at Hilo Town Tavern / 104

Survival / 105

Spirit Lodge, Saturday Night / 106

Elvis / 108

Say Hi to Willie for Me / 110

Listening to Neil Young with Ed Steck / 111

for
Cassidy

*This is overwhelmingly real,
but our lives go on nonetheless.*

-Tim Dlugos

New Poems

A River for Huff
for Albert Huffstickler

I think of you often when the coffee has
cooled, and though this cup is chipped
and the country itself gone to hell,
I do believe poets belong everywhere
and can do some good. I believe
the needle stuck in every heart stems
from the words first sharpened by
poets in small doorless rooms. You
say you were only looking for a way
out, mistaking your pen for a key.
I say we never make mistakes. Today
my wife has left me with a pot
of the dark stuff, two cats, and a bottomless
ache. She asked for the river and so
the river is here. In winter we watch
its stillness from the window. Have you
ever seen a frozen river from this
distance, Huff? It's the spike readying
to strike the silence in your chest.
It's the first word to pierce the heart,
the first good thing every day.

Sanctuary

I'm happy to just sit here, drink another beer and listen
to you. I should be back at work, but let's leave that
alone. You say you are tired and so very worried.
So many that you love are now at risk. Heavy boots
kicking in doors and lawyer after lawyer, you say.
Factory work, working the fields. Crabbing
on the Chesapeake. All that sweat and blood.
The tenderness of coming home and the fun
when a little money is in hand. Oh dance and dance.
Wheel and turn and fall into the laughter. Hold
her all night and in the morning get back to it.
If you get hurt there will be no food, no light
to love by. So don't get hurt. And when you do
don't tell anyone. Pain is what we share
even if we won't admit to it. I cannot promise
these days will pass. I'd love to jump into the Allegheny,
go down there into the filth and silence, and when
I come up, lungs hot and depleted, know
that each new breath meant a change for the better.
But that is what a young man believes. I can
only listen now and listen as the light fades
and the darkness and your whiskey-sad voice
are all that remain.

The Saddest Marathon Station in West Virginia
for Jason Baldinger

Somewhere just below the Pennsylvania line
a gas station attendant laments, I ain't seen you
up here lately. No, she says in sweatshirt and shorts,
I got a better job up the Taco Bell, as stars flashing
across your windshield splinter like some secret
society of Cadillacs hauling bodies for the border.

Fourteen hours this van has run from that tasseled
shore of the Missouri, the city there decked out
in art deco neons, the old signs gracing the skyline
are inscriptions across a barren page. Surely the poets
who settled that fountain town could teach these mountaineers
a thing or two about unemployment and inertia.

But here the jeweled slopes of home are calling.
Did you notice she didn't even look at him?
Just took a candy bar and left him there alone
in the saddest Marathon station in West Virginia.
Our taillights the closest thing to love he'll see all night.

Words My Father Never Taught Me
for Sam Hazo

I would be hard-pressed to prove this city
existed should it ever disappear. If it required more
than a rusted out street sign and a stained menu
from the BBT I would be out of luck. I could produce
the apartment at 214 S. Evaline in angelic detail,
but it would only exist as words and words
I find are often doubted. Maybe if I repeated
your name over and over I could conjure
my grandmother's house on Negley Avenue.
Maybe Hazo is simply code for Home.
Maybe poetry isn't so much a map, but a chalk
outline at a crime scene, the negative space
where a body I once loved bid this world farewell,
a hollow space haunted by chain-rattling words
like Love and Sorry and Shame. Sam, tell me
that I exist. Tell me you understand. Show me
a city I know as mine. For I am lost and home
is a foreign word my father never taught me.

Erroll Garner at the Ace
for Cassidy Lee

From a third floor window I imagine
I can almost see the cracked black
& white tile welcoming Penn Avenue
to the long-closed Kappel's Jewelers.
Behind the dirt-caked door I see myself
blond as the afternoon sun and holding
my grandmother's hand. It's her day off
and she's come for her paycheck. I've forgotten
their names but the manager's sweet cologne
is always there, like the feel of a fresh bag of hot
cashews from the stand inside Sears on Highland,
floating through my memories. Hard black hands
bent the bands of wedding rings and tapped
the names of young brides into the gold until death
they part. Like the sound of Erroll's piano, a copy
of Gemini spinning gorgeously on the turntable,
that hard, bright music of metal upon metal
is an echo of the harder things to come. My wife says,
Frank Lloyd Wright as the claw-foot tub fills
with hot, clear water. A small Clyde Hare photo
of three women sitting on a bench is there
above the bottles of gin and whiskey and soda.
The sound of that too, the rushing, pounding water
is a rough surface across which Garner glides
like we glide down to dinner counting
the Teenie Harris prints as we go. Here's one

of Roberto Clemente and his beautiful boy.
And you are my beautiful boy. Here is the world
of your father, this world now gone. The August heat
of East Liberty is different now. You'll never feel
it this same way, your legs tanned and sticky
with sweat, small hand tight in the grip
of your grandmother's, and all the faces on Penn
a mystery and wonder like all lives everywhere.
Now I'm bare-assed and high above the city,
that lost land lovely and dirty and sad
in the deep summer humidity. The sound of a piano
worked by Pittsburgh blood clotted upon the dying
breeze and something like a bird hard at the job
of survival and happy as hell for the chance
at this new world.

The Departed
for Larry Levis

Behind the corner gas pumps someone has blessed
the late morning traffic with a mural, a procession
of skeletons sagging against the eastern face
of a remodeled bar, and back of that McConway
& Torley adds its daily share of poison to the air.
Larry Levis once intimated loneliness is undignified
then whistled a Billie Holiday tune into his own
last darkness. Did he slip his feet into the water
before walking away? Did he see these white
doses swallowed up by the trusting sky? In the end we all
become timid accountants tallying what we gave and all
we still owe. I come here for the noise and rabble
and a glimpse of that white horse. I sit at the bar,
lose myself not in the drink but in that river of voices.
Like the other three this river is contaminated, too
but still I long for it and, though years will be taken
from me, I bury my head in that deep red rushing.
If I'm very still and listen closely my father's voice
will surface like flecks of gold in a prospector's
sieve. It's true those who remain must carry the departed,
Larry. And there is no shame in that. Hell, it's good to know
there's something I still have to offer the so many
I have failed. Alone as I am now there is much work to be done.

An Old Man Poem
for Bill Gainer

You said to get in touch should I ever need
an old man to do the heavy lifting, if I ever
found myself in foreign lands with no command
of the native tongue like in Kansas City, or if I
found myself stranded on the PCH and
the only kind Samaritan had that Charlie
Manson vibe. You also said the rumored extinction
of the carrier pigeon was just bad science
and they still dotted the skies over the Tenderloin.
I only had to carry the right seed, and a lot of it,
to curry the favor of a bird in hiding. Your advice
is mostly inadvisable, Bill, but the truth is
I could sure use your hand on my shoulder
right now. Oh Christ, there's one wild son-of-a-bitch
running loose in my brain, and Bill he sure could
use the company.

The Suicides of Paris

It's spring again and the suicides of Paris are all the rage.
Twin sisters bound at the wrist and twined by bad blood
were pulled from the Seine. Here the Allegheny

is dredged and a stray B-52 becomes the new museum
    attraction.
Think of it, an atomic bomb right there in the river. Look
at the bodies on the shore. Taste the ash on the air. I know

an artist who insists on leaving the erasures apparent in his
    pencil
sketches. They fetch good money in Shadyside galleries
where we feel the ghost lines glowing. Old home movies

of Lawrenceville are shown. The colors of the neighborhood
soak into the shoreline soil. Men in old Steelers jerseys
and sometimes bare-chested dive from wobbly canoes,

their children delighted and terrified by the enormity
of the river. The mothers are witnesses to infinite hunger
and the white sky droops across the faces of white buildings.

All of it the same smooth white of scars across the wrist
floating there on the dark and heaving water.

Acts of Contrition
for Jason Irwin

The bell tower burned down the same year my father busted his
    right wrist
chasing a wobbly foul ball right off the garage roof near Butler
    and 62nd
and the bells we hear this evening chiming Vespers were first
    recorded
closer to Cincinnati than to Morningside Avenue, nearer the
    whispering
west than to these brown choppy waters that take tugs and all
    the scrap they haul,
concealing them in the shade of metal towers, dark as Washington
    in funeral regalia
who said too much suffering is never a good thing for any city,
    his cold eyes
falling across the scabby wet knee of Millvale broken out in
    blood and beer
and the warning we hear watching the bruised hands of Maxo
    Vanka in prayer,
and just as it took only one good day for James Wright to declare
    the impossibility
of death so this one good shot of whiskey absolves us of the
    burden of our days,
as you become a shadow now fallen across the still surface of
    your glass, happy to risk
the undertow, foolishly assured I or some good stranger here is
    strong enough
to carry you should your will give out.

Burning
for Margaret Bashaar

You are reciting poems as the Braddock Avenue trees
litter pink buds all over, or perhaps you are dreaming.

These million floating poems carry your full heart
in every red line. Over there they still make the stuff

to raise bridges and skyscrapers, they forge the steel
we sign this earth with. Someday you and I will share

such rare wine words will stain our tongues. Our dreams
will glow like the red melt of a mountain, this world's core

spilling from our mouths beautiful and burning.

Graffiti

Stunk of cigarettes lit ages ago and smoked deeply
as though the filter was an extension of the soul
and your soul awash in confusion and endless
late night Eat n' Park coffee was one more sewer
in this city flooded and capsized in the wake
of teenage sweat, the very last lights of which
pulsed and reddened, the naturally ghost-faced
ached in the extreme and begged for your touch
as dancers beat each other into bloodstains and still
called it dancing and the great, awful sounds
wrecked you for life, the ringing still righteous
and vibrating your powdering bones as out on
Baum Boulevard we suck in the chill winter
and one time maybe kissed in our big black coats
and all around fat flakes of snow scattered
like atoms before the immensity of us.

Panther Hollow Inn (1992)

After working the Carnegie dock all morning
they'd commandeer the same line of crumpled
stools they held down yesterday, lunch break
carrying well into the dinner hour, while upstairs
the owner did a bump with the guys from the neighborhood.
That summer I'd ride to work with Velmirovich
who never once looked at the road but kept up
a rapid assault on the radio, punching buttons
like a flyweight over and over, never once hearing
a song through to the end. He'd find me in the afternoon
spiriting me off in a cloud of Camels. The guy to my left
sold Ritalin by the pill. The little one with the ant-trail
mustache said the 15-year old summer girl he was screwing
was crazy, stole his hubcaps, knocked out the taillights
with a rock. She spent the night drunk in front of his mother's
house demanding he come out. Later I hear him at the
    payphone,
baby, baby, you know I love you, baby and the sickle
of a summer moon was stuck up over the roof, the owner
up there hitting it again.

Asylum
for Kenneth Patchen

When the sky opens up I hurry for the bus shelter
hoping for some kind of asylum. I've nowhere to be today
so I'll just watch the rain. Things sure have gone to hell
just as you predicted. I hate it when you're right.
I hate how the drivers here ignore the One Way sign
and just do whatever they want. I've seen some near misses
and I've seen honest to God tragedy. Everyone is
so damn careless. I'm no different. I drink too much
and avoid my doctor. I'm going blind by the way,
did you know? Pretty soon the shape of everything I love
will be a memory. Maybe that's good. Maybe I'll appreciate
you more. It doesn't rain all the time here, but I only really think
of Pittsburgh in the rain. Just as I only think of you
when the bus doesn't come and the rain becomes snow
filling the arc of each newly lit streetlamp like a riot
of the dispossessed.

The Mystery of Faith

It's not the mystery, but what is on the other side
of it that calls to us. Not the sun retreating
in a fusillade of raging pink, but the quivering
darkness of some fried solemnity that draws me
to the shore. Once the air was so thick with grit
and ash my mother's hands came away from prayer
blackened as an ingot. Every morning I throw open
the bedroom curtains is another kind of prayer.
The cat's tail jerks this way and that and still
our street never changes. I would cry after
those early confessions. Performing a suffering
I had yet to truly feel. The old priest endured
the shame of watching my small shoulders shake
as I sobbed in the nave. Each Sunday after I watched
for the Lord's sleight of hand, the tell-tale vibration
of the altar boy's arm and the not-so-mysterious chime
of the proclaiming bell. The river embraces the
wrecked shoreline and no one pays attention.
Someday soon the skies will go black again
and my clasped hands will carry the stain of my days.

The Lie
for John Grochalski

Here is where the wind wrapped its hundred strong fingers
around the throat of her grandfather's pin oak and ripped
it from the Ohio clay, where the roof of the house
buckled beneath the forced embrace. It's Independence Day
and the damage brings tears to my eyes.
The milk-white sky and this small yard, prowling
with crows, pay no mind. It all just goes on. The laughter
inside the house sounds brave from this distance. Nothing
like the sound of the world holding its breath.
Maybe the mosquito crawling up my hand is the perfect
    companion.
Maybe this sun getting hotter by the minute has something to say
if only I'd just listen. It's possible these days will pass
like all the others with only us taking notice. Everything
my eye falls upon could not care less. My eye lacks the resolve
of a summer storm. All I do is watch and hope for the best.
It's the lie I want to believe.

Apology to John Dorsey for Missing His Reading

Let's blame it on being middle-aged. Let's say
the languid bodies of the crowd kept me
from coming. My own starched skin prickled
at the touch of the sun and my eyes at full-squint
could not find the way. Let's say I am a liar.
Strange to think we spend our time this way,
but writing these poems is no different
than drinking at the bar. It's in our blood, I suppose.
It required generation upon generation of bullshitters
to contort my tongue in this precise fashion. Perhaps
you suffer from this same genetic malady. Instead
I made my way through the dry brush and potted
re-bar to the water. When you get down to its level
it's black as mirror backing. Nothing but shadows
in there, and the garbage floating down from Blawnox.
Look all you want you'll never have to confront
your own image here. The muck just won't allow it.
On days like these I prefer the river to our poems.
If I had to see myself, as I so often do in your words
I don't know how I could return home, go back to my wife
and believe that yes everything will work out fine.

Looking at Hokusai's The Great Wave of Kanagawa

Looking at Hokusai's The Great Wave of Kanagawa
what is the mountain and what is the wave?
Perhaps it is foolish to think there is any difference.
To bury the dead is to celebrate the living after all.
Laughing at tragedy is the only brave thing I have ever done.

We take the curb like a couple of Lawrenceville drunks
laughing and tumbling into the pebbled concrete.
Oh, look at the sky won't you. Blue
is an unnerving color. The color of overdose and rot
and the eyes of your first love. When I was twelve

we moved to our first house and I painted my room blue,
laid blue carpeting from wall to wall, and played the old tapes
of my old music for hours with the windows open
and the screens not even in yet. Every song was blue
after that. All the sounds I heard at night too. If you stare

at something long enough you begin to see the hidden shape
of it. If you watch your son on an ultrasound you will see
your own fast moving future. I would lay
here with you forever watching the roaring sky push
a mess of clouds around. I would stare into that terrifying

blue for as long as you asked me to. Your need and the cold
wind watering my eyes so very blue in those very first pictures
my father took of me.

My Father Was a Kind of Country Song

The radio hovers somewhere between jazz and blues
as the hot sauce drips into my eggs and I work
on my second cup of coffee. It's early enough the world
is mostly quiet, but for the construction crew raising
a new collection of condos. The sun butters itself
across the sidewalk tables and a breeze kicks up.
They never do turn off the neons in those bars across
Lombard, just leave them buzzing all day long.
In there where the furious smoke of the anonymous
glazes every surface there is that rare jukebox, tarnished
as a stack of old pennies, haunting the shadowed corner
and the beer-spill. If I close my eyes I can hear it call.
The tinny old speakers sounding like washboard scratch.
How many hearts entered here broken and left the same way?
This floor's been paced over, this stool worn down
to a pencil nub. Wherever you are now you are walking
into this bar. Setting your cigarettes down you empty
one glass after another. The fire in you finding release
as you smoke away the day. You like the hard stuff:
Possum and Hag. And keep it going until you've turned
your pockets inside out. I see you now
unsteady in the doorway lighting another
and looking at the street where I'm just a memory,
a trace refrain to another old song you used to like the sound of.

Dreaming Still
for Karl Hendricks

Sharing a few beers as the dusky half-light drooped
in from Penn Ave., I failed to see the crack, a sliver
of blood-red thread that would soon open
like fault lines will – unexpectedly, disastrously.
This continent split, rent in two leaving the living
to helplessly watch you in your Funkadelic t-shirt
now captain of an unsteerable wreck. Here we float on,
foolish and diminished. The horizon looks injured,
bullied and sucker-punched. We all suffer
in your absence. The bruise spreads up my arms
into my wife's dreams. In her waking life she watches
as I fade into the words that lead nowhere,
foraging for language to sustain us as we move
together in silence. Someone say something, please.
Say I am dreaming still. Say this dream is done.
Say his name, say he is here. Say this poem
has done us any good at all.

South of Pimlico

We were all laughing when the vulture folded
its wide wings and walked the length of the street
south of Pimlico. Like a black-coated landlord come
to collect the rent he ignored the rage of the dogs
and the incredulousness of our friends. The low
clouds of the Baltimore sky and the stink of the
neighbors' garbage shared a similar lack of
concern, and the day just continued in spite
of the chill tucked like a sick child into the base
of my spine. Last night we shared the familiar
darkness of the basement bar where we decided
to marry. It felt good in the shadows. It felt like home.
The rain held off and the beer flowed the way
we like it. In the morning we disappeared
into the crowd under the overpass buying
strawberries and asparagus, drinking good
coffee and enjoying the disintegration of our
selves into the mob. We were born anew in line
at the pickle vendor and made a pact sealed in the red wax
of our secret names. In the Inner Harbor the tourists
slip through the chain stores like drops of water down
a windshield, each wet mouth hungering
for that first taste of crab meat. Here Maria's
laughter is sweeter than all of that, and even
this doom, feathered and ravenous, in the street
we have borne witness to cannot change that.

The Skaters
for Anna

Once we were the skaters, thighs hard
with muscle, on the ice at PPG Place
the sound like viols aglitter with crystal.
And next we were the ice itself
eager to be cut into and written upon
by the frenzied lines of strangers.
And once we were holed up all afternoon
in a tacky downtown bar even though
you weren't drinking then, and you met
with seltzer my toast to us and the new year
approaching. And once we were the liquor
sticky on the Polish Hill tile, and your name
was a new flavor on my tongue, and you
took me shot for shot and said yes, this is
for me for life. And once there was a hummingbird
loose inside you and we listened together
to that mad heart, tiny and strong, happy
in the music we have made of our shared blood.

Almond Way
for Scott Silsbe

We made heroic work of a few six packs
while warm breezes skirted through
the screen door and pushed salt crystals
and breakfast crumbs around your kitchen
table. One of the great Irish poets
of our fathers' time crawled out
of the grooves of the black disc
dizzying around your turntable
like some Belfast haint rattling
it's jazzy chains. You never cared
for flutes, no matter the season,
even with summer ensconced
on Almond Way and the tinny ripples
of the river running up the alley.
We could have been anywhere
but this is where we'd chosen.
You who have walked the black shores
of Paris and Kalamazoo invite
this dirty river into our talk
and even though you say Berryman
and Brecht I hear Allegheny,
oh Allegheny.

Distraction
for C.K. Williams

Charles, forgive me for I am distracted and the peculiar
    wolfish light
of your poems has been refracted by my moony frame of mind.

My inattention to the miniscule detail daubed into the grain
    of the page
I'll compare laughably to Hamlet's inability to kill a king,

to the howling winds of Elsinore keep, to the brazen windy farts
of an off-, off-, very off-Broadway audience, say the Bowery,
    say Fayette County.

The rain pearling at the window and the pliant resigned
    mews of a white
cat in a denim lap wage a hushed war conscripting my wife's
    arsenal

of potted plants and the relentless sizzling explosions strafing
    the skillet
under her expert hand and the lovely red rain of spices that
    glimmer

down into the wide black eye of the dinner pan; the peppery
    aroma
redolent of her humid breath and the late summer nights in
    Baltimore

when the curtains were left lashed and the neighbor across
 the way
got a good look at our shared red skin. Charles, let's pinkie
 swear

someday to share a summer solstice, hold it between us like a
 document,
the terms of my surrender bold as the signature of a founding
 father,

your words measured as a tailor's tape no longer groping at
 the smooth
face of my negligence, my dreams no longer of Anna but of
 those lesser vagaries of art.

Listening to James Taylor at 40

This is a different kind of degenerate art.
Like pouring an entire beer into your own lap
it settles the blood, and just as you'd never
want to spend the night with a mope
at the Monroeville Mall food court you'd never
mistake Frank O'Hara for Franco Harris.
It's like ordering cocktails under the grand stairs
of the William Penn and receiving tap water in return,
or taking the river walk to work
while a boatload of highschoolers
drowns in the Allegheny.
Not as much fun as it could be, but even so
better than you were led to believe.

Trouble

Much like the silent film star so impossibly unaware of the
    bank safe
precariously dangling thirty stories above the tender bloom
    of his wild

dreaming brain, the tiny veins of rope snapping one by one
    like synchronized divers
curling musically into the void, I go about my business
    lackadaisically

trusting the ambivalent mathematics of some invisible hand
is randomly in my favor and the cop's billy club will not
    smash open my head;

the errant spark of faulty wiring will balk at burning down
    the home I love;
the wet cough will prove only an irritant and not augur a
    vast calamity

compelling my doctor to walk me through the benefits of
    chemotherapy
and the necessity of draining our bank account. How can
    you stand a fool like me?

This is a city of steep staircases inconceivably slick with ice
    the whole year through.
Every day each of us naively hopes for the best. Even this
    morning I said I love you

knowing very well the trouble that will bring.

San Francisco
for Lawrence Ferlinghetti

I was there in '96 with the woman I loved.
I lost her the same way men in their twenties
lose everything that matters,

by believing I already had everything
I could ever need. In our borrowed house
across the bay she would play Miles Smiles

each morning and we'd watch the fog
approach our bed, the large window
showing everything

but our futures.

Ida
for Adam Zagajewski

I remember a Polish jazz combo I once saw in a movie
about Jews and nuns and suicide. It was after the war
and the band played in basement clubs – bass, drums,
a tenor sax. It must have taken place in the early 1960s,
I remember they mentioned Coltrane. It could have been
1939 or 1944, though, for all the city could say. Warsaw
looked as though it would flinch if you reached for its hand,
like it would turn and run if you opened your arms to her.
It looked the same as the sky this morning in Pittsburgh,
as if color hadn't been invented yet. And neither had
compassion. We trudge through the sideways rain
and we are out of rhythm. My wife is reciting
the mortality statistics for women giving birth in America.
The numbers sounding no different than a litany of
the war dead. We've been trying to get pregnant.
The world needs more good people, my wife says.
She says things cannot continue this way. We have
a responsibility. I think I hear the barest whisper
of that beautiful song through the downpour as the high
wind cuts through the outstretched arms of bare trees,
or it could just be the crying of the bombs
as they start to fall.

Hemingway's Cafe 7.10.18

Two quarters on the bar top and the leisurely drumbeat
of a stranger's hands adding counterpoint to a midweek
doubleheader. I'm here for the air conditioning
and the bartender's disinterest. I'm here because there's
nowhere else to go. I'm not yet drunk enough to be
so maudlin, and yet. Too often I'm overcome
by all the junk in my head that I could pass on to my son.
Looking at the state of things, though, I suppose
that should be the least of my worries. I take a moment
every day now to ask whatever the hell is out there to ask
that he isn't too disappointed. With me, with this country.
With the foolishness that passes for our days and all of the lies
we insist on telling ourselves about ourselves. The other night
I dreamt he was here with me at the bar. Just a boy and proud
to be with his father. He tried to steal sips of my beer,
and his mouth was wide with so much loud laughter. My son.
What a wonderful dream. There are children right now lost
across this country who may never see their fathers
and mothers again in this life. They are made to sleep
in cages. Some are beaten, some abused. Most simply ignored.
All are weeping. In my dream my son is kind. He is generous to me.
Not once does he ask, What did you do to stop this?

Pouring Ketchup from a Fresh Bottle of Heinz 57

Getting the angle just right requires countless slow afternoons
with the sun knocking right at the window, your elbow up
and out at a measured 45-degrees and a calloused palm flat as
the brim of your grandfather's favorite hat, the upward blows
should be firm but reassuring like a final punch to the arm
of a friend you will never see again, the slap on the back
to someone choking at the table next to you, a life saved
and unwasted, a future released unfurling while
the tv signal cuts in and out and you ignore the phone
trembling in your pocket and the things you do not want
to hear that someone will insist on telling you.

The Photograph of Jay Dantry at the Entrance to Jay's Bookstall

Your standard issue khakis crisp as a street corner
and all the young men around you. The shadows
of aircraft are small ghosts at play on the ground. And
your eyes the same as ever betrayed the memory
of an old joke, the joke you would still tell as a sign
of love. Where have those dance halls gone, Jay,
that music that held you together so far from home?
We never truly appreciate the things we should. Harry said
your last words were I'm sorry so you must have known
even in the fog of successive strokes since sorry was something
I'd never known you to be. I still walk past the old storefront.
They sell lottery tickets and loose tobacco. They've refurbished
the whole place and it's clean and well-lit and there's
no old man at the counter to tell you a joke or toss you out
on your ass according to his whim. No porno mags and no
Shakespeare. No photos of the famous keeping your company.
No more glorious mess. It was the mess more than anything
that confirmed you were alive. The hundred times a splinter
from the broken window frame stabs your palm, the endless
parade of cockroaches brazen enough to loiter in the open,
every time you ran up the basement stairs and dust rained
down from the rafters, each afternoon salad oil stained your pants.
You were alive. We were all so very much alive. The city
was gray and dull and filled with ugly snow, but our breath
in the air was proof we were, in fact, here. And now that
you are not here I am sorry too. Winter is just about over,
but I can still see the pale play of my breath lingering
and your voice telling me I am here. The shadows

of the neighborhood trees and my shitty moods are only a hint of those ghosts almost solid on the tarmac and ready for flight, ready with a terrible joke and later the music already striking up in your ears, the arms of young strangers waiting, the world as I will know it years and years from there.

Bunny's Hasty Tasty Pancake House, Dayton, OH
for Lee Morgan

We don't like the pancakes we like the eggs over easy
we like the Formica tables names etched
in the deep white scratches we like the bottomless
coffee and the fine bottoms of waitresses
we like Elgar and Toscanini the way they
slide into the booth with us and get us all
to quietly hum along we like the view of the
parking lot full of Lincolns and Caddies and the passing
traffic and how there's nowhere else we need to be
we like Bunny and how he says he's
left-handed in both hands we like
how he still likes Ike and keeps his photo
over the grill a glossy layer of bacon grease
making the general's eyes shine we like the shelters
Bunny built during the war for the orphans
and nuns out of big mahogany boxes
and how he dug the tunnels under the floors
to help warm their dirty bare feet
we like that we don't have to talk about the war
very much at all we like that we're here and not at Bill's Donuts
we don't like Bill and neither does Bunny.

North Beach Offering

I will accept this one day. I won't have a choice.
The way I spent my time in San Francisco not finding
the Saint John Coltrane Church,
but staring for hours into the hatched face of Paul Klee's
Stachel, der Clown. I took coffee at Vesuvio's
and Irish beers there too,
while across the alley every phoneme
of every mad word riding my bloodstream
gathered dust and gestured to the rough hands
of men older even than my father.
We offered what we could to North Beach
and dined with one hundred librarians,
butter caked on their croissants
and the little white plates of the cafe
were chipped pedestals
where the late afternoon
discarded the sun.

This Train Won't Run

The basement window kicked in is still
a sound that wakes you more than thirty
years later. The clicking on of the steam
heat and the banging radiators. The car
gone and no food. In all the houses
fathers are angry or asleep. You know
all of this well. Stolen bikes and blood
in the dirt of Natoli Field. The day
Claudio chased Frank down the alley
with a steak knife, eager to feel
the give of adolescent flesh.
Chickie stuck her head out the top floor
window, called your name and laughed.
She thought you were her grandson. The day
the T opened they advertised free rides,
but sent us all home when the train
wouldn't go. You live your life with water
on all sides but have always known yourself
as landlocked. Our youth did none of us
any good, and the ones who left are the ones
with something almost like grace.

John Lee Hooker in Juneau
for August Kleinzahler

Lombard Street in Portland is a ways from Alaska
but Pittsburgh feels even further from here.
Watching the street life, a middle-aged man
in tan overalls, the woman inked up and down
and lovely. I set your book aside and look
deeply into a dark beer. I'm alone and happy,
but still I wish she was here. Sunsets
out on the timber line are rapturous
and glow like a clean knife at the table.
I suffer from a sad disease and the need to tell
you about it. It's the same as tired fingers
stretching for the right chord and failing. Oh
this sun will not relent and I cannot hear
the Willamette for all the traffic. In Alaska
a poet rushes the stage and the music
must stop. In Pittsburgh my friends go on
without me and I wonder if that's for the best.
The beer has been flowing and I haven't once
refused it. When your head goes swimming
the blank page is just one more white cap eager
to crash you down. I can't say I earned this life,
but it does go on in whatever city and any skin
these words wear. The blood just continues.
The judgment is my own.

This Vicious Year

Perhaps when we are gone we will enter into
the beautiful history, as O'Hara called it, but
I fear it's vastly more likely our current civic
disgraces will forever keep the door barred.
All the coins I hoard that never find the palm
of an outstretched hand, every daub of color
so indistinct and ill-defined the museum goer
never notices, every clear sky day you can't
be bothered to look up. It all goes on the cosmic
ledger. I may be lousy at math, but even I can see
how the tally goes against us. Ah, but here in this darkness
and anonymity I am comforted. This jukebox here
brim-full with throbbing, inconsolable hearts
is a badge on the breast of our better graces.
Patsy Cline and Ronnie Van Zant may have
punctuated their lives in the breakage of gravity,
but nightly we listen as they rise and take
the heaviness of the day with them. Billie Holiday
plants a bloody, endless forest and demands
we climb our way out. Up there we loose
a torrential rain of tears, but who's to say
the resultant flood isn't cleansing? And Elvis,
my God… The common belief is the universe
is cold and empty and this speck of dust
is the only game in town. And what have we done

with this mathematically improbable honor?
What will you do with the next hour, the next day?
Here in this bar on such an ugly night in this vicious
year whose will be the next aching voice, the last
absolutely precious thing we can all agree on?

Never Let Go
for Frank O'Hara

Amazing how tired I am, 3pm a Thursday.
People keep talking to me unsolicited,
and the bar across the street is owned
by a Republican draft dodger. There's no relief

to be found. How did you do it? All that energy
and enthusiasm. If I didn't need the paycheck
I'd never leave the house. Last night
we had drinks with my favorite poets. Today

it doesn't seem to matter. For no good reason
I find myself thinking about Balanchine.
And then I'm wondering what Sun Ra is up to.
I know they say he's dead, but come on.

How could death hold purchase on that man?
I'm thinking of the time I watched my wife
swimming off the North Carolina coast,
my feet in the soft relentless surf. Out there

at the end of the earth the sun would eventually
set, but right then it was like the sun and myself
would just go on forever. The sound of her
in the tide a reason to never let go.

Our Li Po
for Bart Solarczyk

Sometimes a bear will growl and poems erupt
from its belly hirsute and gorgeous. Sometimes
a man just wants his pipe and a blank page.
Often enough sweet smoke rides a night breeze
cresting above the suburbs inviting the attentions
of a fucked-up muse. Bart, you've been wrangling
the wet reflection of a summer moon so long now
you've gone and grown a fine pair of ink-soaked
gills. I'll wait here in the boat while you make
one last dive for it. The morning news will say
how a great grizzly was found on the ocean floor
furiously scribbling poems, the meat
of all meaning stuck in his glowing teeth.

Apology

Sorry we had to meet this way, our mutually bony elbows
    colliding
at the bar. I hope the russet splash of pinot upon your sleeve
is as fondly remembered as the brackish stout that enlivened
    my lap.
These are our beautiful wounds. Here in the drab gloom of
    October,
the days each curtailing a wink sooner than the last,
we have each other. Headlights will illuminate the familiar
    journey
home, but for now this silently shared embarrassment
in the dark will burn beautifully as a secret sun
and the next round, should we ever meet again in the spillage
    of life
my friend, is on me.

Home

My wife is planting trees in the neighborhood.
Cherry and Redbud in the cold fogged-in morning
up here, and later will track the dank odored
earth of Stanton Heights down our hallway
and stain the bathroom rug with the black
grit of years. A blessing on our home
recognized by our cats and regaled
by their yowling selfish selves.
This good house with its relatively new roof
and shaky plumbing sheltering
our hoped for family and keeping the Pittsburgh
rain from soaking our drunk friends, this
harbor of dreams on a hill where all are welcome
and sleep mostly comes easy will stand I hope
just this side of forever. Like those trees
in the green expanse of Sunnyside School,
etched into the hillside like words ever defining
themselves anew. The green smell of those words
on my wife's hands when she touches me and tells me
I am home.

The Rumproller

There is a great banging coming from inside the brewery
while out here in the sun my blood knocks at the blue
ceilings of my veins like an irate tenant in the apartment
one floor down unprepared for that first blast of Lee
Morgan's trumpet as The Rumproller kicks off its assault
on the funk deprived asses of Butler Street. The outdoor
benches are bare of shade and the spring-shocked trees
of Allegheny Cemetery, absent their green regalia
stand there in a stupor. Goddamn, it's really gonna happen!
The winter has donned its shabby hat and shown itself
the door. They arrive like Romero's hungry children,
the sun and this last day of March crawling around
their faces, ready for renewal, eager for sex and the gauzy
delinquent decisions of warm days and warmer more
spectacular nights. A nod is all we need to say we survived.
The world didn't end and that was not a guarantee.
Touch my hand, put your hand to my cheek. I'm so happy
to see you again. The sun is shaking its beautiful fat ass
all across the sky. Etiquette demands we do the same.

Selected Poems

A Poem for Jeff Who Is Far Away

Do you remember the way a city tastes?
All gas and yellow

That's how poems look

A little color there, a little blood
Is that a cataract or did someone sneeze?

My kitchen drawers are full of take-out menus
and music is always playing

She unpacks her clothes
while the cat sleeps in the bathtub

Real families are not gifts of blood
We build them from the best of what's available

It's the only important thing we do with our lives

Oh and we write poems
and people who can't write poems drive cars

I don't mean to brag, but Jeff
I crash cars

Fifth Avenue Poem

Watching at the window
Fifth Avenue appears
strung with paper rain

organized and sent falling
by tiny hands

cars go splashing
through the pulp

writing poems on puddles

this world is torn from a dream
then torn again

it used to be this way
a single sentence

now confetti
tumbles in the street

Denver Poem
for Tara

Take care when you leave tonight
all that you take is all that you want

remember the feel of our bodies beneath the barlights
a-swim in you I float in neon
barely breathing and happy

are all the nights in Denver like this – a
needle dropped, the sweet vinyl spinning

now I know where blue records are born

oh honey, the city I return to
never took me in arms wonderful as yours

Pittsburgh

Without faith
we merely sigh

and resign ourselves
to the day

avoiding its stare

I made a bible
of those soft
brown maps

and attempted
a liturgy of streets

and even with such solid proof

empty lots
phone books
cafes, banks
the old statues baking in the plaza

I never completely
believed

you are real

Coleridge Street, December Ninth

Jessica, I can read the weeks,
every year to come, writ upon
sky – black and soundless

stars don't fall, they're dropped

I see the tiny hands working
cutting the strings just for us

all over town people are watching
for some sign everything's not a mistake

even one small light sweetly flying down is enough

now look what we've done

look how the kids cannot help but smile
on their lips wishes wait to break free, in their eyes

nothing but the flashing wake of our somersaulting star-fall

Poem for Yvonne DeCarlo

We learn to laugh at the darkness
much too young

the nights are wet and cold

there are noises coming from
locked rooms
we do not recognize

you touch my bare belly
and my every white hair
gets up and tries to leave

I'll turn on the television
for the familiar voices

I'll pull down the moon
to stop it

watching us

our strange dreams
walking around the room

A Poem for Jessica

Falling is my one fear

if I'm not careful I crash
and love, I could not survive that

I know I don't smile
as often as I should

it shows in photographs
and in their eyes

they know the truth

I never write anything
but ghost stories

Gelsomina
for Giulietta Masina

She cannot help
puffing into a trumpet

or pulling faces
for a crowd of penniless
children

one boy in bed, infirm
the sickness under
his skin did glow
lovely as a wedding feast

what can be done but
laze about convent steps
and fizz at the mother superior

pop and dance and parade
upon the cold winter sod

a clown could only ever die
in this rumor of heaven

her song so sad
ages of peasant girls
hum it

while the wash cracks
along the line

After Patchen

O love this is when I worry most

the night comes down heavy
as damask, a curtain of regret
and starsong

O love this world shines
in the clock ticks, burns as the second
hand climbs and falls
diving into the future I fear

my heart of stopped time, a murmur
wanting mostly a memory

I know this body to be a sieve
and you only a phantom
shivering through

O love

Nights at The Cage
for Loucks & Moody

Ah, she's a sweet piece
this table swollen with tumblers
and rich with shotglass poetics

here she comes again & we smile
louder than bums

the froth rides and she kicks
we're swell as a sagging nag

oh, wee!
let's whinny, boys!

one more love poem
to the sharp swallow
and the self-immolation

go bury your face in the jukebox
and dream 'twas a silken thigh

hey wow!
o fuck!

how can anyone make their legs move
and still find the car

how did Silsbe put it?

ever see me wrestle
a parking meter?

Ray's Marlin Grill with Scott Silsbe

Tucked in the corner
back by the men's room

one dollar grants three plays

whatever the night
no matter how hard

the drunk
you've disembarked

on that ship solely
made of empty

domestic brews
you drop a buck

in change down its throat

begging at the buttons
best as you can

foraging from the sound
something more solid

than the memory of the day
no music played

and she left, leaving
no songs

untouched

Ciao Marcello
for Fellini

The sea is eternal
or so the song goes

thus what is borne
within all water
is eternal

you and I
my love

a puff of air
and we are

vanished

Bloomfield Bridge Tavern, Tuesday, 7:26pm

I prefer a polka when I've been
drinking . The way things are
going, might as well go ahead
and install an accordion between
my ears. I have the place to myself
on a Tuesday night. The rain
coming on cold. Honey, I could
use your kiss right now. We've been
too long together this bottle and me.
I guess I miss you, and I never
thought I would. I miss
my father too, but I won't
mention that.

Silky's Pub, Sunday, 2:10pm

I don't believe anything will ever quell
the deep satisfaction of taking a meal
at the bar. The plate of food steaming perfume,
perspiration beading the glass and my forehead.
Alone on Sunday afternoon and no worry
of churches disgorged of penitents eager
to proselytize and point fingers in my heretic face.
The bartender, Scandinavian or some such, eyes
the ink pooling across this page. The poem, to her,
upside down, incomprehensible. The poem to me,
as I go, the same. Ed Steck is working
somewhere. Jeannie taking time with her mother.
Smokey Robinson is on the radio and nothing
could be better. I fear August and strangers
who approach on the street. I take one long sip,
then another. The sun stands still.

Poem for Dr. Harry J. Mooney

Those early evenings smoking cigars in the bookshop
basement set a fine example for this skinny kid, barely

twenty and seldom confident enough to string together
more than two or three sentences of talk. It's hard

to get anywhere once you've convinced yourself
there's nowhere worth going. I can't look into the river

and imagine where that river ends. I do, however, know
where this street ends and when this world will end, too.

Like the last page of the finest novel everything will stop,
a breath caught in the throat, 11:00am tomorrow morning.

The Last Call
for Anna

You stroll through the open doorways of bars in Polish Hill.
If you take the bridge you end up in Oakland or possibly the
    hereafter.
It gets harder to tell the difference the more time we stay here.
Tell me again about the stairways that are actually streets.
Show me the illegal magic of a left turn.
Let's break up this machine on the Blue Belt and leave our clothes
    buried under the new snow.
Have you been waiting as long as I have for the moon to bleed
its gold all over Bloomfield?
If we're careful of the ice I think we can make it across
the BBT parking lot alive.
Or we could spend the whole night trying to get Jocko
to eat pretzels from your open hand at Howler's.
Margaret is at Lou's tonight, or did she say The Pleasure Bar?
Well, certainly it wasn't Silky's.
Let's find her before she elopes with the bartender, unless
that will soften our tab.
I suppose there are better ways to pass an evening than taking
on the taps in a thousand bars,
but none of it would be as blessed.
Perhaps it's the church in me rising from out of my skin,
but the low lights and cigarette smoke could be vespers and
    incense.
Tell me, what choir could be holier than the jukebox at Gooski's?

The Pittsburgh Baedeker

Isn't it wonderful I can open a Baedeker and know
The brilliant wool-clad asses of Byron, Voltaire and Dumas
Got down to business on the banks of Lake Geneva

Rutting in the aromatic mud with the invisible
Little lapping sounds like those of a kitten at its milk
The overt suggestions, the red tip of the world's tongue

Tickling at the heart by way of a well-scrubbed ear
And here I am tacking the Allegheny to a white pasteboard
Expressing myself in the precise tones of a busted muffler

Did you know the Eggishorn is the uppermost peak of a ridge
Separating the Great Aletsch Glacier from the Rhone Valley
From here the Alps are breathtaking ducking their pearly heads

Behind K & L Gates, stroking the Roberto Clemente, fingers
Facile as Anton Karas' upon this golden zither, I brush the hair
From your eyes at PPG Place and check my teeth for cervelat.

June 16th, June 16th

It's only right that I should sidle up to the sun and put my lips
  to the ear
& roar to beat the flame that June 16th has come and there
  will be hell to pay
Should the sun take cover under a heavy blanket of cloud
  drifting asleep
To the soothing susurrus. Somehow, my love, I think we're
  solid as the day

Is golden. So what shall we do with the world (cracked egg
  that it is)? Everything
Is yours for these twenty-some hours (O let's add an extra &
  say there's 25
In a day!) and I am also yours, but for so very much longer
  than two sweeps
Of the clock face. The motion of this man will return to a
  crawl, of course,

Become a creak and a wheeze and a fit of coughs bent double,
  but for the promise
We make I won't fear any of it. Only the absence of your sound
  sleeping, your
Joy & sadness, your love for me, you – this is all I fear. But
  not today!

It's June 16th & all that matters is born anew.

Poem Addressed to Jaquelyn Seigle

Jacq, these hard yellow days you never
Get used to. They trumpet around
The front lawn and wake the neighbors,
Get the dogs barking. I've spent many
Good days writing poems outside bars
Watching the old neighborhood and the girls
Who live there now. If we're not careful
Nostalgia creeps up on us like a housecat
Let loose in the yard. And then it's only the drinking
That helps. No one ever tells you there's an airplane
Falling out of the sky and every day you are
On that plane and falling with it. So
I make phone calls and pray for wings. I watch
The sky for fiery debris and for my face
In a cloud. Jacq, I look for your face, too,
But here on the ground where it does
Me the most good.

BBT

In Bloomfield the beer is cheap and here we are
With chairs liberated from other tables and a glassy crowd
Staring up into our eyes. Out here is the bridge and little
Houses beneath it. A ball field gone barren from lack of play
Do you believe in any of it? If I tell you it's all gone, everything
Beyond the door destroyed forever, then it is. And when we walk
Outside all of what you see is just your brain filling in the blanks.

Look, there are little lights embedded in the asphalt here, a beautiful
Long line shimmering with every step and the black sky has got its hat
On, ready for us to leave and bow like a gentleman upon our exit crashing
Its dark brow into the broken sidewalk of your very last dream.

Some Morning

You float from the bed, flurries of sheets
folding into the floor, the cat confident
running a course of desire in and out
all around your little feet as they go

into the kitchen, then to bathe
a sweet fog perfumed of your skin, you
have become the air all around my head

I have an inexhaustible need for these streets
and the wonderful women, summer kissing
up their bare legs, walking always walking

I call to you from out here in the morning
my voice gets lost along the way
all turned around by

the whispering mouths of water
talking all across your body.

The Whiskey Rebellion
with thanks to Jason Baldinger

There is a line stretching from the men's room urinal all the
    way to the
jukebox. It does something to the music, this anxious
    shuffling of human
requirement, the sibilance of shoes sweeping soft leather
    across the pleated floor,
the many lipped conversations colliding,phantom jets spilling
a white wake of suds in your lady's lap.

You must administer the right ammunition to quell the uprising.
Else you are engulfed - arson or amber?

These are the long nights we will fail to remember, the
    nagging nights that
push at the corners of closed eyes. The ghosts that give
    themselves up and go
I am tattooing the tatters of your memory into this soggy
    napkin we call
'poem' damp from the years fallen in floods from such
    kissable fingertips.

Baltimore

We were talking about forgiveness, or we weren't talking
at all and in the darkness of the place I was only thinking it.
What could be more difficult, more required...
but this was merely a scattering of salt, errant crumbs
of unspoken regret – all that shit between the man and me

and you had just taken a long pull on the pint and our friend
was with us from the other town and the two of you were
    talking
not about forgiveness or loss or family, but just talking and
    being
human (what could be more difficult, more required)
while I studied the shapes scratched into the table top – some

approximating words, others their intent. You must have said
something then, or you took my hand and clutched it to your
    belly
and pulled me from the water I could hardly tread into this
    thing
you were building all on your own with a secret reserve of
    wood
and grease. Our friend was back with a fresh round and
    strangers
moved and made noise and touched and when did all of
    these people arrive?

I should probably pay closer attention to this world, at
the very least I should look it straight in the eye and be honest
although subterfuge is hard to shed. Perhaps removing my
   jacket
is enough, after all, we're among friends, and it is getting hot
   in here.

Dawn Powell's Diaries

You take what the weather gives and never once
offer rebuke, nor admiration, the world is the world

and this is not the world. You pocket churches and hospitals
like pennies, tour the Hebrides via the alley off Morningside

Avenue, and pray for a bar not filled with reams of stupidity and
bullshit, just good bourbon. The chances of this are slim as

the river in a season of drought. We talk by way of telephone.
You describing an engine perpetual in its grinding of all things,

self-aware and hungry as hell. I ask what you've been reading
and the line goes dead. Soon after your letter arrives:

These are vicious days to live in. The bastards love it here.

If I try very hard I can see through tiny spaces in the wall of
heavy summer leaves, and from this place I can almost see you

moving from face to face across the crowded measure
out there in the twinkling paradise.

For Robert Frank

Robert, remember the older pair from the bar after the parade
and how that dim room lit entirely by a lonely little jukebox
somehow made the women beautiful and precious to us as we
hung the day on the glass hook of the night and tilted our ears
at their heavy mouths, cheeks and lips pale full, wet with our
    money
Robert, and I recall the quality of your talk when
you invited the two ladies together to dance, blushing and
    busting laughter
against the old walls and the photographs of the old people still
hung on those walls and maybe you didn't notice but I fed a
    five's worth
into that smoky juke and with an elbow against the warped
    red lights I leaned
and loved you, Robert and watched the one in the fading blue
    shift spin
out of your arms, eyes an explosion soft with so much
    gratitude.

Poem for Anna

It is 11:40am, Saturday
sweet puffs, scatterings

of dust, risible on car vapors

splash dryly, explode
in the beaks of birds

are scraps we've torn

out, telephones are ringing
all up and down Craig Street

the ghost of last night's beer
goes with me

up museum steps
the paste white cloud,

blue crepe de chine.

Pedestrian Ceremony

I never understood your casual bedlam,
the heartbreak offered for free.

This is snow on a summer's day,
a pirate signal from the mystery lake.

I'm working the radio in the dark.
Stabbing antennae at heaven we

Hope for the best.

Your pedestrian ceremony has made the hit list.
Expect a bullet in your sleep.

After Too Many Beers with Baldinger

After too many beers with Baldinger
the room glows like a deer's eye,
bright filament of possibility
birthed in the fizzed brown amnion
of a Baltimore stout. Streets below Stanton
hum, operas of ballfields chirp out
weedy melismas, somewhere sweet oaths
are sworn. This benevolent elision of need
furnished by night, this rising architecture
of sleep, this invitation to abandon
oneself to the deep stuff of drunktalk,
the collective mumble of the slumbering
neighborhood a polyglot patois we interpret
by laying ear to table and taking tongues in hand;
inebriate night, distillery of dream
soused and legion is the language
sung by twilight stumblers such as we.

W. Eugene Smith

Our disappointments keep us human,
little victories tempt us to become believers.

Never believe.
But trust the city will give new reasons to get out of bed in the morning.

Someone at work will say something and it will be amazing.
Someone will say, Let's have sex, right now!

and you will.
Every light bulb burns out eventually.

We keep new ones in the closet by the front door
that way the dark never lasts long.

And though we stumble, arms outstretched
the walls turning to bodies under our touch

the brief mystery of it is enough to convince us
there is no such thing

as time enough in the light.

Congress Avenue Bridge, Austin, TX
for Don Wentworth

This city wears a face in the formation of its birds, yes
they beard the sky an unbelievable black; a voice, too
in the fold and flap of feathers breaking for flight. The cry
an insistent scrawl of claw across bone. Don,

how do we sing? I haven't the heart for this heat.
I haven't the stomach for the spice. What right have I
to walk this bridge and watch an unbroken line of bats
    brown with urgency
multiply and mark this world as its own and satisfy

myself that I am of the same line. What brotherhood I imply!
How nervy taking a razor to a stranger's wrist, drawing
my heart into that mix. A thief of names is that what I am?
And what are you, my friend, other than some beacon in
    the woods

shooting small signals into space. This place is an empty
    room waiting
For the telephone ring. Knocking at the door there was no
    one to let me in.
Don, I wasted an entire afternoon walking around in a
    house not even
for sale. And here is the house I wear on my hand. Someone
    has blacked out

the windows. Someone has moved the furniture. Oh, where
    is the map when we are
truly in need? Don, we are weird! The bridge is filling with
    anticipation.
Grackles have given voice to the trees and small boats circle
    in the river.

What are we expecting to happen here? The nightly
    amazement as creatures below
Wake for the hunt and pour themselves into the dusk
as we hold our breath and we try to hold on.

Poem Addressed to Jonathan Moody

Jonathan, can we agree on heaven?
We've all seen maps to places that don't exist.

Poems are just more maps
leading us out of here.

Stanton Heights

All around us middle-aged men mow lawns
and small gray cats yawn on doorsteps.

Aisles and aisles of autumn afternoon
and hardly a brow furrowed in worry.

No homes here ever go empty or without
Some sense of, well, maybe it will all be okay.

Your clothes come off easily and you are right
the beer is better in our underwear.

12 E. Read St.

Your note said, *Don't be late and bring some beer. Dinner is assured!* and standing there in the hallway's damp light
I did feel assured – by the delicious curves of your southpaw
script, the coming chill of another shaggy season

and the threadbare carpet straining to keep separate
my eager feathered feet and the creaking hardness
of this too solid living. I throw cold bottles in a bag
and fairly fall down flights of stairs. I am undone

and remade, like some old scraggle of a grandfather's sweater,
by thoughts of you in your tiny kitchen, cuttings of onion
tomato and mysterious roots & things - I know not the names
–
dipping our quiet loving talk in perfumes of black earth and rain.

The sky has that proud look about it – it's ready to burst! There
comes from the street so many sounds and voices! A rage of
    living!
Baby! Listen o listen! I carry in my wallet little wraps of words,
promises invisible to our eyes but love they are so obvious to
    this heart.

I Am Not Kahlil Gibran

When I worked at the library
this old hippie said,
*Read Kahlil Gibran's The Prophet,
read it to women, give them poetry
and they will drip into your bed
like warm summer rain.*

And so
like an asshole
I wrote poems

in the library basement
nearly foaming
under the big steam pipes
wrapped and sealed and still
sprinkling asbestos
in my hair.

The creaking fishing boats
of far Lebanon
smashed in the torrent

of my churning seas.

The Old Stories

There are only so many times you can tell the same story
pretending you do not see how it will end. Imagining
there was another way for it to unfold. Seeking fresh ears
changes nothing. I wonder what we will tell our children.
And our children's children. I wonder if we are even capable
of opening ourselves in that way. When I wake before you
and quietly move through the house, it's not ours anymore
but some foreign place with a climate of its own, with ways of
paying for things we haven't come to yet. I tell you there is love
but often I am not certain. I haven't thought of it in years
And that is as it should be. This place is warm and dark.
Soon you will join me here and share this with me. I have
not taken a new name, but still I am different.

Heaven
for Bob Pajich

We only come here because this is where our fathers came
to shake off the day's dust and conjure a way to dream again
from all these ripe bottles and bad jokes, all the easy stuff.
And why not when everything else comes with such a heavy
price. Here you can still find foamy pints for $2, here
we still call one another friend. Out there are the wives,
the children, and debt. Why would we ever go out there?
I can see the whole world perched on this stool and I gotta
tell you I want no part of it. Some days someone walks in
with the paper or asks to change the channel to the news.
He is not-so-politely told to leave. There is no time here.
Nothing happens by design. It is wonderful.

Fix Bayonets

We're trading stories in a Baltimore bar and
earlier today I was drinking beer from the can
in a sunny DC yard with a wolfhound happy
to have my hand curling through his coat and I'm
remembering our friends in Pittsburgh and thinking
about watching the ponies run at Pimlico,
and your sister is somewhere thousands of feet
above Ohio and Seth is on the metro, and there's a real breeze
driving across Ortanna, pollen drizzled on the sky
and housecats out in the big yards when we watch
not one but two tourists fall off the rocks
at Little Round Top and I wonder if it's the enormity
of the killing that took place here, all that death
staining everything the same sorry color even though
the park guide assures the crowd this is where the war
was won as an older couple from deeper in the state
tend to the wounds of their boy, and Chamberlain
gives the order, Fix bayonets!

Ruth

My grandmother kept a few records around.
Scratched, dusty things she would sometimes
play on summer Sunday afternoons with chicken
spitting in the pan and gravy brownly bubbling,
or sometimes late at night sitting in the kitchen,
the small white stove clotted with grease,
the bottle of Canadian Club she kept under the sink
with a jar of silver dollars and Kennedy coins
out on the table in front of her.
whiskey and water her drink of choice
in a chipped glass, long white cigarette,
sometimes a slash of lipstick across the filter.
Dean Martin or The Ink Spots filling the house
around her. Sometimes after a few she would make
phone calls, and sometimes the only voice she needed
was Dino's.

Mannish Boy
for Bob Pajich

I will never know what Muddy Waters
thought in his green suit and chunky gold
ring as his leg leaps up and crashes down
and his cheeks shake any more than I
could say on such and such day
Einstein had a hard-on watching
the students pass under his ivied window.
And I might as well admit I used to spy
on our neighbor, a woman known to prepare
meals in the nude, the brown medallions
of her areolas still bring a wonderful pain
to my nethers. So it should come as no surprise
as we sit on a brick porch in East McKeesport
or stumble out of some bar on Electric Ave.
or when Nathan, rolling a cigarette in the booth
at Nico's, leans in to laugh at something
one of us has said, and someone in the other room
yells, Fuck! Shit!! at the lottery drawing
that I wish I could say how any one of us
got here, but really it doesn't matter
and anyway there's a green suit out there waiting
for each of us eventually.

Good Noise

I'm beginning to worry there is no good noise
left in the world, no sound to spur and spark,
nothing to catch the thread of the day and yank!
We could get in the car and go looking and maybe
find something worth the effort, but probably no.
When the storm stabs at the metal roof the cats
run for cover and the rest of us jump in place.
We listen to old soul songs and sometimes we dance.
Sometimes a new hand takes its place in yours, sometimes
bodies still fit together in amazing ways. And when
my wife is gone I think of her in that familiar way
and then I cannot say over drinks somewhere, I was
never surprised, everything turned out how I knew it would.
Because I knew nothing. I suspected nothing. I was a creature
of so little imagination a block of gleaming marble
was forever a big rock obscuring the view
and every moment in the company of these people
seemed a chore. That smallness of vision arrives again
with the weight of the ordinary, familiar as these
Sunday afternoons here.

Identifying Trees

These are not palm trees bending in the window.
Our hillside ripe with the season–Black Cherry,
Black Locust, Ailanthus–not so pretty as the southern
species. Enmeshed in heavy tangles of knotweed and
the wind makes the whole green wall move and talk
as though the neighborhood was dreaming it.
And in this dream of ourselves we are not so weak
and the summer sun holds sweet invitations.

It's easy enough just to go and never return.
I know a man who did this as though it was his job;
a clock to punch calling out from some southern city.
He will never see the view from our kitchen window,
never lay up late into the night like I do listening
to the snores of my wife and our too many cats,
never hear a Canadian wind again as it converses
with the doomed Ash white as fresh bleached sheets.

I have no excuse for not tending more closely
to the needs of our trees, and to the garden. And
to you. Expressing intent in a poem is meaningless,
like trying to look up through this snarl of foliage
and find the right constellation, the true north
we hear in our blood, that right providence
burning out there in the inevitable dark.

Summer Town

The weather here demands new and obscene synonyms
for oppressive and muggy. The heat unbuckles
your belly and slips a hand inside. I quit my job
just to save myself from walking to the bus stop,
to stay inside and watch the cats pant instead of purr.
We count our many coins and plan to move north.
We look at maps that resemble the foreheads
of all our grandfathers. We place orders for delivery
but can't peel ourselves from the couch to answer the door.
The poor kid leaves our dinner on the step, but even
the raccoons will not venture from out of the trees
for free pizza. My ancestors made their way here first
by boat and later by train. I think of the wonderful breezes
they must have felt and the spray of ocean water cool
in the afternoon. I watch the neighbor's kids
splash in a kiddie pool and think we could probably take
the little bastards in a fight. You say talking like this
gets us nowhere. And I wonder at how beautifully
Siberian nowhere sounds, how nowhere is exactly
where I want to go.

On John Cheever's First Listening To Joni Mitchell's The Last Time I Saw Richard

It would be years yet until the man was reduced
to shallow whispers in the library, and his work
calcified and grown crusty with all the –ism's
of the classroom. But here in the sounds his daughter
so generously shared he could see all that coming.
His face so hang-dog and sleek must have cracked open then
in awful recognition. And anything he might have said
to the contrary would have been only pretty lies.
He would pass as one more dreamer from the room, descend
to an underworld of his own design and fastidiously undress.
The suit coat first and proper, next the deep blue neck tie.
His crisp white shirts were always hung on a wooden hanger
hooked carefully to the low-hanging water pipe. And now
at the typewriter he continued to peel away the costume,
this lame finery of brown-spotted skin, until at last
he could see himself laid bare upon the page—one more
terrified man, a swimmer far from any discernible shore,
gulping at the bottle as though somewhere a pocket of fresh air
would surface and allow him passage from this place, rising
into the music he could still hear far, far overhead.

Poem For M. Callen

If we had the time I would tell you about the night at Chuck's
we passed around a book of poems and in small,
beer-spillingly tragic voices read to the man the words of his
long-dead friend, and then I would say, You should have been
there. It was your kind of scene. And maybe then I could
tell you about all of the times I bent myself over pen and paper
and worked a dredge through my memories hoping to score
a direct hit on some childhood trauma and salvage the waste
of it, dragging the soaking thing on to that most barren of shores-
the blank page. And how each slow scratch of the pen
sounded like some roaring thing set loose from the zoo,
each halting curve of an S or C was really just a rope
I prayed would catch to the edge of the cliff so that I could
climb from out of this chasm. And I think you above all others
would understand that, and you would have taken the book
of poems we passed around and turned to the page
emblazoned with your own words, your poem finding its way
into a stranger's work, and there in that warm place,
the meowing of many cats floating in hand with the drunk talk
of our friends, you would have spoken some truth we needed
desperately to hear. Our own secret words singing from your
mouth as the summer sun sunk down inside of itself and the
leaves, just beginning to brown, obscured all the light.

Old Women and Their Old Dogs

Old women and their old dogs are everywhere
in this neighborhood. The slow distress of their
movements an affirmation of the inevitable.
They linger at corners, gossip with the long-widowed
woman who threatens strays with poisoned bowls
of cat food, click up and down the street
in evening hours seldom pausing in consideration
of our neighbor's nightly throw-down with her daughter
and the police who crowd her porch have nowhere
to put their hands. I cannot see these old women
and their old dogs without my own errant understanding
straying to this nagging, grievous knowledge–one of them
will die and leave the other in stunned desolation.
This will happen to us, too. In the shadow of this imminent crisis
I can only hope for some amazing mishap involving modern art
and an old-fashioned amount of whiskey, or something
so nonsensical the survivor can only tell it
like some wonderful punchline.

Omar Moreno

What could that have been like, stadium rimmed
with Serbs, Poles, and the Jews, too, happy-drunk
beside big-armed Russians and mellow cats
from Homewood, and the lathered Irish wails
from the men's rooms, and each one with the balmy
music of your name cresting the tides that poured out
of wide open mouths crisp as a sluice of spiced rum,
highly seasoned as down south homecookin'
in that cartoonishly green pen, swell of rivers in the offing,
children wobbling in the stands fetching beers for shit-faced
fathers raw red from the cheering, aloft in the nosebleed
seats with one hand to God's hem and the other down
the old man's pants and not a care in the blessed world.
And, of course... Of course I miss my father. How could I not
when I dream up such a gorgeous scene of deep summer
in the boiling city of the Golden Triangle, that tender palm
of this clement universe, a warmth and a wonder
and my father away out in the wilderness, Omar
please keep that man safe.

Celica

My parents' Toyota Celica flecked blue and silver in late summer
sedentary in the supine afternoons as my father slept

the white vinyl of the passenger seat sporting a shiner
the tiny black-eye of a cigarette burn

and the backseat sterling for a boy stretching out
sinking in waves of stereo noise

suburbs bending like guitar strings in the unwashed windows
tracing beads of light in the dust motes shuddering

across my drum-sticking fingers
streetlamps showering strange shadows every-which-way

and the shredding keening knowing shatter
scratching its way through tiny speakers

all those songs my stunted inheritance
as much as bad teeth and nearsightedness

something like my father's voice swampy with cigarette smoke
a vanishing thing signaling from some lost certainty

the sort of single-mindedness suffered by children
so longed for now behind all these surrendered years

My Mother Looked like Stevie Nicks

My mother looked like Stevie Nicks when we were all so much younger
and she wore a tan bathrobe fuzzed softly as sunlight filtered
through the crocheted sieve of kitchen curtains, orange and floating
over a full kitchen sink of suds and gravy-stained dishes and embossed silverware;

and she wore a t-shirt in the yard off Negley Ave. powdered green and plush
serving up the Bee Gee's Main Course across her chest as she ran after the dogs
and I sat on the step, my hair white and wild the way it was then, with this same expression
my face has carried like a favorite tune into my forties, freckled then and mostly free from worry.

This hastening distance can only traffic in the barely audible echoes of our voices,
some pale and sorry excuse for the true music bound lovingly by black sweeping hands,
forever circling and forever entrenched I see my mother when she looked like Stevie Nicks
and I hear that music sweetly tattooed upon time, graceful and tragic

and still the best song I've ever heard.

Yinz

Is the sound of our one-eyed cat, claws plucking at the
    screen door,
contrary as a fur-coated John Cage at his prepared piano

as cooing pigeons pucker and crimp their filthy wings
and explode from the breadcrumbed stoop in gales of shrieks

and white stinking shit, spooked by toothless leonine yowls;
the sound of my one and only fist-fight as two

supremely uncoordinated boys in coke-bottle glasses
swung and whiffed, swung and whiffed

then pushed and kicked the big soft belly
of the loser writhing in the Sunnyside School parking lot,

loose gravel spraying from under him
with every pendulous exertion of my angry flying limbs;

the sound of city buses expectorating in the rush hour heap,
and wild Ruthie at the pharmacy punching in your digits,
    first straight

then boxed; and the way the bartender pounds a bottle of
    Iron so hard
suds slide down the neck soaking the want ads; and is this
    the sound

of the ocean, too, and your expectations sinking in the
    indecent gurgling tide.

A Belated Poem for My Wife's 30th Birthday

O Christ how I want to write a poem without sputtering
in defeat only eight lines deep like some asthmatic
    jackhammer.
Surely it's lovely somewhere still
and isn't that remarkable enough?
Are these days unworthy of mention simply because they feel
    so similar?
When I say last Monday it's clear I could also mean Tuesday
    three months ago.
If I didn't have to pay the water bill I wouldn't know the 25th
    had come and gone.
But we will always have your birthday to set our watches by.
And I know Five Easy Pieces is 98 minutes long
and The 400 Blows is 99.
And somewhere in all that time unspooling a life can be lived.
That last time we sat together and talked in a movie theater,
as couples came and went around us,
you said you would come to where I worked just to look at me,
to watch me move and talk to people I appeared to know,
and sometimes act stand-offish or cruel.
You thought you could love a man like that.
And never before have you wanted to call a stranger
    sweetheart more.
But time passes and here we are.

And what's strange is we used to sleep in different beds in
    different houses.
And isn't this worth the effort of commemoration?

Isn't this worth all the time we have remaining?
Here in the dark quietly together.

Salsa Night at Hilo Town Tavern

Along the wall in straight-backed chairs they wait
their turn with the only man in town who truly
dances. The husbands and boyfriends relieved
at the bar, happy for a surrogate while the ballgame
goes; and the dancer deejays his own private disco spinning
a new record for each delighted lady, while in the tourist
shop doorway another meth-head beds down,
and I worry that dengue has claimed my blood, and the
saddle road waits for our morning drive to the dry side;
and all over the island is a singular hush,
but for the mumbling behind closed doors
and the rats in the rafters of our rental. Here
where the clouds reach down and stroke
the cheek of the land I wait for your return
from the ladies' room and feel how young this
world sometimes is.

Survival

When we talk about money what we are really saying is,
    I am so afraid.
The retired ladies at the bar talk about Medicaid and the
    election.
There's been another shooting and that abandoned house
    finally burned down for good.
It's easy to believe that every day death is winning.

Just because we share a six-pack in the neighbor's yard,
it doesn't mean we know each other.
Watching a baby take her awkward steps feels less like a
    triumph when she hauls off
and kicks the dog laughing.

But at night sometimes we say the word love and it isn't
    something abstract.
Down along the hillside there are deer standing in the road.
In the morning we'll know if they survived.

Spirit Lodge, Saturday Night

When in doubt return to what you know best:
the gorgeous dark eight steps down
and the violent gaze of an archangel.

This warm lacuna dim with blurry voices,
and the boys in the back baking up pizzas,
flour dandering their beautiful beards;

the corner vending machine advertising smoke and coke,
and the cool contours of a cherry red chopper announce
themselves like the last band to ever play The Decade.

Like the advent of winter's first freeze
the streets of Lawrenceville are glazed sweet with the stuff,
and old Allegheny Cemetery keeps its secrets stone-still.

Under the sagging cloth of early January
you say you could drink the bottom out of this town
and still have room for one swallow more:

more of this black beer beading the glowing bud of your lips,
more of this swirling organ aching as a broken femur,
more of this dance floor dotted and luminous as a million
    freshly-minted pennies.

The Spirit Lodge on a spectrally quiet Saturday night grants shelter
to all the spooky shit that goes bump in our brains,
holds its arms wide in welcome to the demons of our damned
   foolish decisions.

We share so much and say so little sequestered here,
the new year creeping across Butler Street
calling our names and pointing to the clock.

Elvis
for Rich Gegick

I knew him the same as you, the same as I know this ash-
   toppled table
and the thick whorls of lacquer we skate beer cans across like
   a Minnesota lake,
the air in here like something you could take a pick-ax to. His
   voice in our ears
sharp as that ax and big as our futures once must have looked
   to somebody.

And you say it wasn't what he sang, but in the end what that
   voice desperately reached for.
Sometimes only as persuasive as smoke, but every so often
   impudent, expectant, and
worried as a new father; sonorous as seabirds feeding in the
   richly purpled sunset.

Out there in the cresting whitecaps the incessant crashing is
   God at his most articulate,
and here we can hardly be bothered to listen. But some nights
   I press my ear to the wall
and there is such a gorgeous rumble coming from the other
   side my eyes go damp.
I know that sound of outstretched hands beseeching, the
   sound of men delirious for love.

It's the same as a southern boy grown well beyond the
    bounds of his own flesh;
all sense of self sweating out of him, evaporating in the
    hideous stage lights,
but for one tender moment of discovery in the face of
    oblivion that tells us it's okay.

Say Hi to Willie for Me
for Jason Irwin

There's a statue where Second Street meets Lavaca just as
    there's a red vinyl booth
where Penn Circle has become Centre Ave. again, and where
    the bartenders
are slow with a refill and the smokers must smoke under
    watch of tangled scaffolding.
New buildings are going up in the east end and old places are
    getting new names.
And there are people coming here who don't know anything
    about it.
It's a languid sun that makes summer days like this one.
I remember Texas in August and it was just like this.
I hope Texas is kinder to you. I was sick from the heat for a
    whole day there.
But they were fast with a Shiner and filled a glass all the way up.
They valued air-conditioning and barbecue and I could
    understand that.
They adapted their world from the Spanish and have words
    alive with music.
I never want to go back there, but I guess it was okay.
But here your regular booth is empty and the mix of punk
    and country on the juke
could have been played by you.
It could have been one of your poems on the men's room wall
    above the toilet.
I was definitely someone's idea of art and I guess it was mine too.

Listening to Neil Young with Ed Steck

I agreed to meet Ed in Oakland to talk poems or work or
    whatever
nonsense we could gather up between us and let sift from
    these indigent
hands of ours into the thick summer weekend, but instead
    I walked the
mile or more to a bar on Liberty and waited, my sopping head
and underarms happy for the air-conditioning, and when Ed
    spilled
in it was quickly decided we'd pool our money and fill the
    jukebox
solely with Neil Young, and so spend our paychecks and the
    rest of the day
drinking beer from big pitchers and enjoying the music and
    the consternation
of the gathered grubby patrons as not one nor two but an
    endless carousing
chorus upon chorus of that Canadian warbler descended like
    a winter's front
snowing beautiful coke-fueled bilge all over the barroom
    blocking out the sun
with Bruce Berry and danger birds and Brando, but finally
    Ed could not resist
the challenge inherent in ascending Sugar Mountain over
    and over, piling remembered pain

111

one pebble at a time into a brave alp we could only meet
   with our own streaming tears,
openly weeping and not nearly drunk enough to explain
   it away, expecting nothing more
than for each of us to step from the peak and plummet or
   soar as we so needed.

Kristofer Collins is the publisher of Low Ghost Press and the books editor at Pittsburgh Magazine. He is the co-host of the Hemingway's Summer Poetry Series. He lives in Pittsburgh, PA with his wife Dr. Anna Johnson and their son Cassidy.

www.ingramcontent.com/pod-product-compliance
Lightning Source LLC
Chambersburg PA
CBHW022007120526
44592CB00034B/703